The Colors of a Woman

Shannon Johnson

authorHOUSE®

AuthorHouse™
1663 Liberty Drive, Suite 200
Bloomington, IN 47403
www.authorhouse.com
Phone: 1-800-839-8640

First published by AuthorHouse 2/10/2009

ISBN: 978-1-4389-2797-8 (sc)

Printed in the United States of America
Bloomington, Indiana

This book is printed on acid-free paper.

Table of Contents

Introduction

By: Shannon Johnson

In her novel, *Their Eyes Were Watching God,* Zora Neale Hurston described women as the mules of the earth. I think she meant that women are often overworked and may be disregarded by men in society, but I have a different take. I reviewed some facts about mules, and I was floored by the similarities between mules and women. The first fact that I found interesting was that mules have a very distinct bray. Although they try to imitate the bray of the male parent (the donkey), they usually end up with a unique sound that is a combination of the whinny of the horse '(the female parent) and the bray of the donkey'. I think women do the same thing. There is a unique voice within each woman that is both masculine and feminine. Women are forced to be both assertive and submissive at different times in their lives. We have to be careful not to be overly emotional for fear that our hormones will be named as the reason for these emotions. At the same time, if we are too stern, we are named "bitches" and dismissed as "acting like a man." Therefore, our voices have distinct patterns that can soothe babies to sleep and command boardrooms.

Aside from our unique "brays," mules and women also share similarities in structure. Mules are marked by having a very straight neck, with very little curve. I find it encouraging that an animal known for carrying heavy loads performs this job with its head held high. Women seem to share this trait. Centuries of suppression and oppression should have caused women to see themselves as second-class citizens. During slavery, women not only endured the same back-breaking labor as their male counterparts, but they were also the victims of countless sexual assaults. However, the world has to acknowledge the resilience of the female sex. There are a plethora of female leaders throughout history who prove the buoyancy of the female spirit. That spirit was modeled in my own family. My grandmother would often come home from cleaning other people's houses with a spotless apron and a smile on her face. She taught me to have pride—the type of pride that comes from feeling secure in yourself. That way, no circumstance can make you bow your head.

In addition to being hard laborers, mules are known as stubborn creatures, but this is not true at all. Mules seem lazy because they will not put themselves in danger. While a horse can be worked until in collapses, a mule will just stop. The "stubborn" streak is just the mule's way of telling humans that something is wrong. In the same way, women have had to yell to the world that something is wrong. Women have put their feet down and stopped in their tracks to tell society that a change has to come. This stubborn spirit may be misread as "bitchiness," but it is necessary to keep us from collapsing under the inequalities of the world.

This pride also relates to the one area where the mule outshines the horse, and that is its jumping ability. Mules as small as fifty inches have been known to clear fences as high as seventy-two inches. These jumps are not from a galloping approach, but from a standing start inside a marked area. This is truly a remarkable feat. Similarly, women have had to overcome hundreds of years of oppression to attain the strides for equality witnessed in modern times. The rights to vote, equal pay, and equal access to job opportunities are just a few of the hurdles that women have cleared and are still preparing to clear. And like mules, women have not had a running start. Instead, women are oftentimes steeped in the miry clay of sexism and oppression, which has to be shaken off before clearing these hurdles. That is a remarkable feat as well.

The final comparison between mules and women that struck a cord was the unique colors of a mule. Mules can be any of the colors that either horses or donkeys come in, along with some unique variations of their own. Some mules often have extremely loud patterns, with spots enlarging or "skewing" in variants of dark and bright spots. Like a mule, a woman's life is colored with bright hues and dark spots. Women have multifaceted experiences that give off an array of hues. While reflecting on my life, I have seen the dark valleys and bright peaks, and the colors seem to reflect all the hues of the rainbow. That is why I wrote this book. I wanted to share my colors with the rest of the world and hopefully inspire other women to create some of the bright colors, while using the dark ones as a base.

Chapter One
Moody by Nature

<u>Adolescence</u>
Moody and confused
Zits outline my discontent
Full of highs and lows

My favorite things

Candy necklaces and bubble gum,
McDonald's fries and an orange soda,
Saturday cartoons and sun-filled days
Make me smile.

Sunday mornings and Friday evenings,
Snow days and holiday weekends,
Fried chicken and candied yams
Make my day.

Weekends with my dad and weekdays with my mom,
Grandparents tickling my knees and
My brother coming home for winter break,
My favorite cousin spending the night and
My favorite show premiering
Make life perfect.

Daydreams

I sang in front of millions of screaming fans.
I danced like Fred Astaire with a Michael Jackson flair.
I played every instrument and taught Prince the keys.

I solved problems around the globe and brought order to the
U.N.
I brought food and shelter to poor people and gave them power.
I brought Africa from third world to the third power.

I made the president laugh and vacationed with the pope.
I had front-row seats at every major concert in the world.
I appeared at major sporting events and outran the players.

A star, a singer, an elected official,
A humanitarian, comedian, and dancer—
All of these titles came easy to me
As I daydreamed under my pink canopy.

Child's Play

We played outside until the sun went to bed.
We ate candy until our stomachs hurt.
We laughed until we forgot what we were laughing about.
We were carefree.

We wore mismatched outfits and forgot to iron them.
We picked up caterpillars and fed them leaves.
We fed lollipops to ants and watched fireflies as we fell asleep.
We were fearless.

We watched TV until we memorized the commercials.
We sang the same song repeatedly until it finally came on the
radio.
We waited to hear the ice cream man's tune and ran three blocks
to buy a vanilla cone.
We were persistent.

Nothing scared us in the world except our imagination.
Nothing was impossible, and everything seemed easy.
Too bad we had to grow up.

Growing Pains

Why can't life pause at eight,
When a bad day means a heavy rain
And you're forced to watch cartoons inside?

Why can't life pause at nine,
When great days are filled with roller coasters and funnel cakes
And you don't have a thought about the cost?

Why can't life pause at ten,
When girls and boys are basically the same
And hormones lay dormant,
Not causing any tensions between the sexes?

Why does growing up mean a loss of innocence and
A gain in fatty tissue and heartache?
I guess we'll never know.

Too Ugly to Cry

What happened to that tiny frame?
I used to jump and tumble with no bra to restrain.

My bony legs are filling out.
My once thin thighs are now stout.

My breasts are budding and my hips are spreading.
Cellulite usurps my thighs.
Where is my body heading?

Acne and growing pains fog my thoughts.
Hormones and preteen crushes make me petrified.
I would weep in my sorrow, but I'm too ugly to cry.

Forget You, Bitch!

I walk to the corner store to get little girl things.
My thoughts are enthralled with Popsicles, teen magazines, and penny candy,
So I don't notice the car drive up to me.

Three guys, filled with testosterone, shout to get my attention.
My baby face is overshadowed by my growing breasts.

"Hey, girl! What's your name?" they yell.
"I'm eleven," I answer.

They ignore the age and yell about my frame.
The thoughts of penny candy scatter away with a bit of my innocence.

Fear tells me to ignore them, so I walk away without turning my head.
In defeat, they shout as my L.A. Gears quickly flick lights onto the ground.

One block of being ignored finally proves a point.
"Forget you, Bitch!" they yell as they drive away.

Now, I've lost my appetite
I didn't need ice cream anyway.

The Girl in the Corner

She sat in the corner that they told her to sit in.
"It was just a game," they said.
Hitting and kicking work in sports,
But this game required her body.

She was weak, so they called her any name they wanted.
She would just cry,
And that made them laugh.
If she complained, everyone would call her a punk.

So, the punk stayed in the corner.
She grew up in that corner,
Only wanting to be their friends.
She started to pretend that she wanted to be there.

I have to admit, I called her a few names.
Who wouldn't? She was so pathetic.
But, I also held her when no one was looking.
She was so pathetic.
She asked to die, and I tried to help her.
It didn't work.
Someone told me to pray for her.
I did.

I finally told her mother about her pain,
And she wept for the both of us.
Her babies,
Her baby,
Me.

They Said

Try this,
No, that!
Smoke weed.
Maybe crack.
You ponder.
Then you're confused.
Either way, you lose.
Cool kids make reputations.
The reputations make them cool.
Until school is over,
Then everyone calls them a fool.
Wise kids are called names.
These names make them nothing.
Either they learn to ignore it,
Or they believe the names mean something.
You decide to be the punk,
Take the punishment now.
No wild parties or sleepovers—
Just the possibility of coming out on top, somehow.

Discovering Self

Pick or choose who you want to be.

Live for the past or live for the future.

Reach for the stars or dive into the sea.

Live happily or wallow in despair.

Choose what you want or waver with foolishness.

Be forever decided or fade into nothingness.

God Said

God said, "Step out of the darkness,

Out of the bitter struggle within your body.

Reach beyond the raging veil of sadness and misery.

Open your eyes to the beauty draped around your smile.

Courage is required to look in the mirror without the eyes of
society.

Slay the status quo and embrace the imperfections

Laced within the fabric of your being.

Be free! Be free!

Choose life and live it abundantly.

Choose happiness and peace.

Greet yourself with patience and acceptance.

Live and be free!"

God said.

Little Me

I want to apologize for all the names
I called you.
I probably ruined your life.

I thought you were nothing,
And that made me hate you.
Everybody laughed at you, and I believed their lies.

It was immature to hate you without knowing your name.
I should have talked to you.
I should have listened.

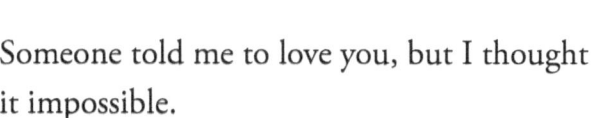

I wanted you to go away.
I could see the pain in your eyes.
I tried to kill that pain and you along with it.
The two of you made me sick.

Someone told me to love you, but I thought
it impossible.
Then, I looked deep within you and realized nothing they said
was true.
When you looked back from the mirror I started to love you.

Now, let me dress those wounds from the past.
Let me dry your tears.
I will hold you and let you mourn your pain,
While you let my heart feel the love you craved.

Chapter Two
Sister Enemies

Sister Haiku
We should get along.
Estrogen can make it hard.
Women love and fight.

Girl Friend

I have searched for you forever—
My friend,
My sister,
But you are non-existent.

It must be overrated—
Friendship,
Sisterhood,
Because it never comes easy.

I make myself available—
Open,
Ready,
But jealousy or envy interferes.

Is that why women can't get along—
Bond,
Connect?
Are we afraid of the similarities?

I Want a Sister

I want a sister, a real sister,
One that calls just to say, "Hey,"
Or visits because she's in the neighborhood.

I want a sister who knows my favorite color
And tells me when there's a sale at my favorite store,
One who knows not to offer me tomatoes
Since the thought of them makes me gag.

I want a sister who invites me to the movies
And tells jokes over casual lunches.
I want the bond and friendship that is associated with
sisterhood.
I am sure you want the same thing.

I crave normalcy and basic emotions from my sister.
Should I wait or hold my breath for your affection?
That's what I want, but then again,
People in hell want ice water.

Stranger

We are strangers, you and I,
Like two schoolmates who never speak
Or distant cousins who meet briefly at a reunion.

We aren't even acquaintances.
We barely speak when we are near.
We make casual conversations to pass the time.

We strain to appear close to one another.
We smile at family gatherings for the sake of our mother.
This façade takes a lot of energy.

We know each other by name, but nothing else.
Without appearances, we could not pick each other out of a
lineup.

We are strangers, you and I,
Sharing genes, but not conversations,
Like stray cats from the same litter.

The Mask

Behind a guarded mask of confidence,
She sits scared and scarred.
She pretends to be put together,
So she coordinates her dress with her makeup.

She lives in solitude surrounded by friends.
Like a chameleon, she transforms and masks her heart and soul.
She pretends that she knows it all,
So she offers everyone advice.

She cannot bring counsel to herself because she is someone else.
She lies through tears, so that people think that she is real.
She is panicked when questioned about any wrongdoings,
So she has selective amnesia.

She is a broken vessel that needs to be fixed,
But she is glued together with discontent and anger,
So anyone capable of fixing her stays far away.
Perhaps, she will stay that way.

Hair

Long, flowing locks cascade down your back.
Soft curls rise and fall like waves in the ocean.
Your glory shines in its ebony hue.
It is beautiful.

People stop and marvel at your locks.
They mistake its beauty for your own.
Those black tendrils mask your equally black heart.
It is deceiving.

Behind those curls and smooth roots,
Stands a woman who hates all.
The tears you cause are overshadowed by that hair.
It is a shame.

Smooth locks and a coarse heart make men love, and then wish
for death.
Looks are deceiving, but they play a significant role.
However, God sees past that, and he will judge your soul.
It is about time.

Girl Fight

Swelling and expanding in my chest,

My heart rate starts to rise,

Pushing tears to the brims of my eyes.

My fists are raised and pounding in the air.

She uses all her strength while tugging at my hair.

Murder is just minutes away.

A crime of passion, some would say.

Love and hate double-dutch in my heart.

Pain and resentment eagerly pull me apart.

I look into the eyes of my sister-enemy,

And I calculate her heartless plan.

God holds back thoughts of homicide.

He gently pulls back my hand.

We are pulled apart, and I plead with anger to subside.

Now, our spirits will battle, seconds away from war.

Love and hate will always intermingle;

Tension looms around every corner, lurking at each door.

Beautiful Girl Haikus

A beautiful girl,
Everything I want to be,
Where'd your beauty go?

"A model," you said.
That was your lifetime desire.
You dreamed of stardom.

They were all in awe.
I was left in your shadow.
Your dreams became theirs.

I was the short one.
Nobody saw my beauty;
I was free to dream.

I had my freedom.
Their attention blocked your dreams.
Depression killed it.

Beauty fades away;
Knowledge lives beyond beauty.
What else do you dream?

Once beautiful girl,
All I wanted to become,
Now you envy me.

Beyond the Lie

Strong,

Intelligent

Woman,

You stood as a matriarch in my mind.

Articulate,

Wise,

Eloquent,

Creative,

You spoke, and my whole world stopped.

I grew up and you evaporated.

Weak,

Immobile,

Dependent,

Disappointing,

Your strength was a picture, a façade of the truth.

What happened to that strength?

You sit in a chair, crippled by life

And disabled by reality.

I looked up to you, and now you are gone.

Downstream,

Downtrodden,

A vestige of what you used to be.

From Another Mother

I was introduced to my sister.
We chatted over coffee, and
Our conversation confirmed a lifetime bond.

No kindred blood flows through our veins,
But our sisterhood is cemented with love.
Our souls are not concerned with surnames.

We giggle over foolish things and sit on the phone
Quietly watching America's Next Flavor of Reality,
Laughing hysterically at our moments of stupidity.

Sometimes we neglect our talks for a month.
Then, we chastise each other for missed time.
We pick up on the last conversation and finish it.

At times, she has mopped up my tears, and
I have combated her anxiety with words of comfort.
We manage to hold each other up.

Our bond makes it hard on the opposite sex.
Any prospects get the evil eye until they prove their worth.
But I would walk down an aisle in any taffeta wreck to make her
day special.

No family lines are intertwined connecting our dots.
No reunions carry our names,
But our friendship is a bond of heavenly proportion that will
last always.

Chapter Three

Looking for Love in All the Wrong Places

Fool's Haiku
Hide and seek gets old.
You play far too many games.
Love's overrated.

Pretty Boy

It's got to be you.
Your hair is so soft, and your skin is flawless.
You're coordinated in the latest fashion, and
You smell so good.

It has to be you.
Every girl likes you,
No matter their age.
I should feel lucky.

It must be you.
If not you, who else?
Will I wait forever?
I've never seen a face like yours.

Love Thoughts (Part I)

I sometimes catch myself daydreaming about you;
I glance in the mirror at my eyes to see if some change has
occurred.
I blush as I think about your scent and the touch of your skin.
Every insignificant phrase that slips from your lips is locked in
my mind.
I press rewind and rehearse our last conversation,
Taking into account everything I think you wanted to say.

My bedroom is transformed into a garden oasis.
White chiffon gently flutters against my legs as I look up at you.
Our hands are joined and our hearts are one.

Then, I am stirred back to reality as a breeze flutters my curtain.
I look back at the mirror, totally in love,
Hoping your mirror shows a similar reflection.

The Gift

Sacred and untouched,
Spotless and pure,
Delicate and cherished,
It is priceless.

Impenetrable and secure,
Locked and kept safe,
No hands have touched it.
No chances have been given.

Many have attempted to gain access.
All have been denied.
No charm could cause this innocence's suicide.

Somehow words seem to inebriate the guards.
A key slips hands; some transaction takes place.
They are fooled, and all is ruined.

Marred and defiled,
Disregarded and disrespected,
Overlooked and overused,
It has depreciated.

Betrayal

You walk on beams of sunshine and dance on rose petals.
A smile graces your face as pixy dust tickles your toes.

Behind your back, rain clouds of deception drown out those sunbeams,
While vines of envy strangle the rose petals at your feet.

You trip over tempest waters that wash that pixy dust away.
Your smile fades with the news of infidelity.

Your perfect love is lost to lust.
Your happiness gives in to mistrust.

You cry to release the pain welling up inside.
You mourn because of the sin and because you ever wore that stupid grin.

Fantasies

Behind glazed eyes,
You fantasize
About infidelity.

All the while,
I smile
Thinking those thoughts involve me.

Your mind is intertwined
With other women's thighs
As you kiss my lips.

I hold you close
And feel loved
Because I am unaware of your cheating heart.

You think it's innocent
Because the sin is in your mind,
Which makes it benign.

I cry anyway
Because my love requires your heart, mind, and soul.

Insecure

Too fat,
Too ugly,
Too short,
Too dumpy.

Plain Jane,
Fat Pig,
Sweet as candy,
But he's diabetic.

I can see why she makes him smile.
I'd cheat too; I'm not even my style.

Too tall,
Too handsome,
Too smart,
Too cool,
He's too great to be my man.
I must be a fool.

Her Plea

I can wear my hair just like that.
I can buy clothes just like those.
I can wear a perfume just as fragrant,
If it will make you happy.

I will be in the gym tomorrow.
I'll lose the pounds.
I can cover the stretch marks,
If that will keep you around.

I'll wear the best makeup.
I'll find new, sexy shoes.
I'll style myself to perfection,
If you'll pick up the phone.

I'll be confident and fierce.
I'll have strength and a regal attitude.
I'll do whatever you want me to.
Whose offer can be better than this?

His Answer

You're the kind to marry,
But I'm far too young.

She's the sexy kind.
I need that right now.

You're sweet; that's why I love you.
She looks so good; that's why I want her.

You just stay here, and I'll be back.
I have to oats to sow, and I'll be back when I'm done.

You're fine the way you are.
Everyone can't be that pretty; you're not made for that.

If it makes you feel better, you can take me out for lunch.
I'll be ready at noon.

My Heart

Stop running in the house!
Don't run past it, because it will fall over.
Stop yelling! It's very fragile.
Stop slamming your hands around it; you'll make it fall.
How many times do I have to tell you?
If you can't take care it,
Leave it alone!

Why did you decide to break something that's not yours?
You should take special care of gifts.
It's shattered, and you broke it.
Apologies will not mend it.
It's trash to you.

Good Morning

I woke up today, and the sun called me a fool.

"He doesn't love you,

You crazy girl; he never followed any rules."

In my dream, you loved me.

You were mine and I was yours.

In reality, you used me.

You were my pimp, and I was your whore.

You could care less about love.

You never heard any of my pleas.

You devoured my heart and soul

You killed the life inside of me.

Now, the thought of you makes me shiver.

I feel nauseous with shame.

I wanted you to love me, and I already loved you in return.

But all you were prepared to do was play games.

I woke up this morning.

The day greeted me with crisp, morning dew.

I washed away a year of turmoil,

Singing, "I'm so glad that we're through."

A Declaration of Independence

You walked around like a king,
And I was the pauper that carried your scepter.

You were the master
While I was a trained pet who carried your slippers.

You smiled at me and thought,
"She's not going anywhere."

You laughed at my tragedy,
Poking fun at my nightmare.

You divided my body and subtracted my mind.
You dissected my soul and expelled my hope.

Every unique thought was slaughtered in your conquest.
I was nothing to you.

But how ugly can I be?
Even dogs deserve scraps.

I had to scoop up the dignity you left in the garbage.
I had to rinse off the hope you scraped into the trash.

I found the beauty you dismissed.
I found the brilliance you ignored.

I found a treasure locked away, and I'll keep that from you.
You'll never get to see the magnitude of greatness in me.

I found a masterpiece that's priceless,
Which I will keep from the worthless likes of you.

Chapter Four

Ready or Not—Here Love Comes

Lover's Haiku
I lost, but you found.
My heart is being repaired.
You came just in time.

I'm in Love with Me

I see my smile shine
Brighter than Heaven's floors and
Wider than the span of the Sahara.
My achievements send beams of glee.
Jesus smiles down on me.
I see me,
Then, I wake up curled in my daybed.

Is It Possible?

Can you wish me well or try to be my friend?
Smile at me and breathe life into my longing lungs.
Laugh with me and share my world.
Hold my hand and see my innocence.
Love me for now and want me forever.
Help me heal and be patient with me.
These rotting wounds will ooze sadness for some time.
Be the one to make me believe again.
Be my friend.

Love Thoughts (Part II)

Lightly, I tread upon this ground,

Wondering if it is hollow.

I shiver with fear and excitement,

Interlaced with hope and doubt.

I smile at your kindness with suspicious eyes.

In your arms, I hold you while holding back my heart.

You caress my face, and my lips start to say, "I love you,"

But I tame them and hold onto those words.

Gradually, we will walk this path.

I tremble on this ground until my heart leaps.

I cannot control it.

This quicksand has my feet.

Enthralled

It's so funny that you're here holding me.
It's so peculiar that you allowed yourself to love, crave, and want me.
You are kind genuinely, and that's amazing.
Now, I know that I never felt happy until I met you.
I never smiled until I laughed with you.
I never trusted until I held you,
And I never loved until I knew you.

His Song

I lay on a floor of despair and agony.

Hoping for death to come and keep me company.

God said, "No" and, instead, sent me a companion.

You walked in, held me, and sang,

"I love you, but how can I make you see love?"

Your song conveyed it.

Your tears made me feel it.

From then on, I wanted to be near it.

Now, I don't wallow in sadness.

Your smile gives me solace,

And I sing because you're near.

When I'm down, I remember your song and feel loved.

The Wedding

Planning took precedence over life.
Five feet of ribbon strangled my capacity to feel anything.
All this planning, and I never planned for my feelings.

The food was catered, but no one warned me about the fears I
must now acknowledge.
Maybe I pushed them under the stacks of *Martha Stewart* and
Style magazines.
They must be buried under the floral arrangements.

Now, they seep into my mind in between thoughts of receptions
and rehearsal dinners.
Will I be the statistic?
Will I be the overweight woman who screams amongst her tears,
"I am better off alone!"?

Will I be woman enough to keep a man?
Or will he stray?
"Because a man is a man," the old women say.

Will I lose my soul in a pile of dirty dishes or amongst the
colored clothes?
Will I be happy, or will I wear the insincere smile of a neglected
woman?
Will I?

All these fears, but there's no time to think—the caterer's coming to arrange the centerpieces.

Losing Love

We created love, and I fell in it.
Did I fall too fast?
Did you run past?

You were there to help me through my pain.
Did you wallow in it?
Did I leave you there?

I became engulfed in bundles of joy.
Did the sounds of her crying drown out your voice?
Did new life kill our passion?

I will remember the love we had.
Will you meet me half way?
Do you love me still?

I will remember you because our love keeps me safe.
Do you still have the key?
Do you know that I still need you?

For Donathan

I see your struggle and admire your dream.
Your workload is never taken for granted.
That's why I use the soft light in the morning.
That's why I tiptoe past the bed as I get dressed.

I see your struggle and admire your strength.
Your frustrations are never forgotten.
That's why I make your favorite meals.
That's why I carefully follow the washing instructions on your clothes.

I hope you see my intentions and admire my thoughts.
I hope my love is not taken for granted.
But, that's probably why you work so hard.
That's probably why you kiss me when you get home.

We see each other in every way.
Our feelings are mutual.
That's why we made it this far.
That's why we're married.

On Coming Close

They say nobody's perfect, but you come close.
A woman walks by, and you don't glance her way.
The lights are on at home because the bills are always paid.
A tear rolls down my cheek, and you reach to hold my hand.
You sure sound like the perfect man.

In your sleep, you reach out to wrap me in your arms.
If you hear a strange noise, you wake to check the alarm.
When I'm sick, you anoint me and pray.
When I'm in pain, you massage me and mold me like clay.
With all these qualities, you remain humble and never boast.
They say nobody's perfect, but you sure come close.

Chapter Six
In My Father's Eyes

Father's Haiku
Other guys hurt me,
But you always mend my heart.
You're Mr. Fix-It.

The Christ

Lambs die meekly and calmly before their slaughterers.

They never fight for their lives;

Instead, they stare death in the eyes and slowly pass away.

It is amazing how this peace causes such a disturbance in my soul.

Your quietness seems to highlight the violent nature of my sins.

Maybe if You would have fought,

I would have been able to muffle the sounds of my sin with the blares of Your warfare, but You never said a mumbling word.

Your quietness leaves plenty of room for contemplation, which stirs up my soul.

I scream out because of Your silence.

My soul echoes, "It should have been me."

I cry out, thinking noise will displace the image of Your disfigurement, but the louder I scream, the more vivid it gets.

So, I weep quietly, and You show me that it takes more strength to be quiet.

In silence, You can stare Your adversary in the face and see past their hostility.

So now, I exalt Your strength and marvel in Your passion.

A Father's Day Song

On Mother's Day, most radio stations are seasoned with
the sounds of songs about a mother's love and her children's
gratefulness, while Father's Day has no theme song.

If you ask most people what their favorite Father's Day song is,
they are hard-pressed to find a song that truly expresses the love
of a caring father.

That thought always saddens me because
I have a father who deserves his own theme song.

If I could sing, I would create a harmony
That delicately described each gift my father has given me.

The melody would paint a picture of the compassion and love
he has shown.
The song would showcase the unconditional love we share for
one another.

If I could sing, I would create the best Father's Day song,
And we would sing it on the way to our weekly lunch date.
We would hum it on our way to the tennis court.

But even though I cannot sing, I hope these words create a song in his heart—

A song that ends with a line like "I love you."

No One Like You

When I was young, every time I got a shot at the doctor's office,

You used to buy me a Barbie doll.

I appreciate that.

As a child, when I felt depressed,

You taught me self-defense and made me feel powerful.

I needed that.

As an adult, you took me to lunch,

Picked my thoughts, and became my friend.

I commend that.

Now, you care for my child,

Gloat about everything she does, and protect her when I'm

away.

I love that.

There's no one like you.

No one could replace you.

You are my daddy.

I'm so happy about that.

Like Home

It takes a strong man to live with someone else's child.

Many men ignore the child and pretend not to care.

Unlike most men, you have embraced the family and made each day a holiday.

Never once did I feel that your house was not my home.

Your Sunday meals have supplied nourishment for my body and soul.

How proud I am to call you family.

How thankful I am that you came into our lives.

Never feel unappreciated or alone, because as long as I am around,

You have some place to call home.

His Exodus For Granddad

Time marches on.
A long life ends.
Sickness seems to prevail,
While mourning cries echo.
But amongst them, I hear a voice utter,
"Come on, Lord! Come on, Jesus!"

Bruised hands reach out to his children.
Their goal is to say good-bye.
An oxygen mask muffles the sound,
But I can still hear him say,
"Come on, Lord! Come on, Jesus!"

His lungs fight for air.
His throat is hoarse.
His voice trembles as he yells,
"Come on, Lord! Come on, Jesus!"

His wife offers him a meal, hoping to comfort him.
"No food!" he exclaims.
"I am going to eat at the Master's table."
He accepts the invitation and shouts,
"Come on, Lord! Come on, Jesus!"

A long life of faith comes to an end.
A son, a soldier, a husband, a father,
A chef, a cab driver, a pastor, and a friend
Enters heaven's gate with a loud bellow,
Calling upon his Lord saying,
"Come on, Lord! Come on, Jesus!"

Now, his soul leaves his war-torn body.
Young again, he tips his fedora,
And he struts on golden streets,
Walking beside his Lord, singing,
"Come on, Lord! Come on, Jesus!"

Chapter Seven

I Never Knew Love Like This

Mother's Haiku
Often forgotten
Never allowed to forget
Ignored and needed

Not You

Society created the idea that two women cannot become close.
They say at some point the women will fuss and fight,
curse and backbite.
For some women this is true, for some women, but not with
you.

You have always helped me, encouraged me, and strengthened
me.
Courageously, you raised me to be more than pretty.

I am strong because you taught me to be.
I am smart because you told me to be.
I am compassionate and caring because you modeled that for
me.

Some mothers shelter their daughters from the world and keep
them from growing up.
Some women do—some women, but not you.

You motivated me to dream, strive, and succeed.
You fed me bowls of knowledge with a side of wisdom.

You poured your brilliance into me and dimmed your light just
to set me free.
You sacrificed to make me strong.

Not all mothers show unconditional love.

For some women this is true, but thank God, I have you.

All You Do

I spent my tender years attached to your hip.
I needed you beside me just to fall asleep.
So, you slept beside me and kept me safe.

I spent my adolescence hiding from my fears.
I needed you to show me how to love myself.
So, you prayed for my salvation and kept me alive.

I spend my adult years talking to you on the phone.
I need you to be my friend.
So, you listen to my ideas and make me laugh.

I will spend your senior years holding your hand.
You may need me to help you with basic things.
So, I will smile with every request and be your help.

I will remember your shelter, your prayers, and your friendship,
and
I will try to return those things to you.

For Grandma

Once soft and tender,

She danced the Madison and rested her arms on her partner's neck.

She was a belle and the talk of the town,

But she was miserable.

Molestation and verbal abuse made her feel ugly.

No pretty reflection could erase that filthy past,

So she hid behind her anger.

She stood fearlessly and watched her husband go to war.

Seemingly barren, she was shocked when four children entered the world,

Partially welcome.

She grew to love her family,

But that growth was not free from thorns.

Feared and hated by some,

She sank into old age and became acquainted with grief and misery.

Little does she know, but her whole family brags about her ninety-five years.

They feel a deep sense of pride about the traits she has passed down—

Her forthright attitude,

Her strength.

They love her in spite of her spitefulness,
Because they understand the pain and depression.
That trait was passed down as well.
They will try to get through it together.

Thinking of Eve

Full of love,
I bathed myself in his fragrance.
I melted into his skin,
Hoping to create something bigger
Than I or He.

A full moon later, blood tests confirm
New life has begun.
I smile at minor discomforts
Excited about what has become.

Thirty suns and moons slide by
And I feel close to death with new life inside.
I pray, and there is no relief.
This is how it's supposed to be.

When I can raise my head and stop flushing my nourishment
away,
An image of new life gives me new hope.
Her blurred profile makes me smile.
I realize God has never left.

As my belly grows and people notice,
My face shines exuberantly.
I wear clothes so people can see
My belly button protrude slightly.

In my joy, men in white coats announce some problem.
Spots and things may mean the end of new life.
I wish for my own death,
But God is not gone.

She moves to show me their prognosis means nothing.
She is fine.
Now, my belly presses against my womanhood,
Signaling her entrance into the world.

My selfish prayers end.
"Do not protect me," I pray.
"Make her okay."
God answers my prayers.

Nobody told me new life was this tremendous.
I am baffled, and my heart breaks and leaps at different times.
I will wait to tell her and remind her that it all started with love.
A love she will never forget and from which she will never be
freed.

Skylar's Song

As soon as you were born, you grasped my hand.
Then, I knew that you loved me,
Even though you were too young to understand that you were—
My beautiful, beautiful, beautiful girl.

While looking into your eyes, I began to cry.
My heart expanded with love for you
As I held you close and prayed for—
My beautiful, beautiful, beautiful girl.

Then I knew that this love could not be explained.
You represented all the good that God planned for my life.
And His greatest gift was—
My beautiful, beautiful, beautiful girl.

You lay on my chest, and I felt your heart beat.
I rocked you to sleep, kissed your cheek, and
Began to weep, overwhelmed with love for—
My beautiful, beautiful, beautiful girl.

As you grow older, one day you won't need me as much.
Hopefully, some part of your soul will remember
The day you came into the world, grabbed my hand, and
became—
My beautiful, beautiful, beautiful girl.

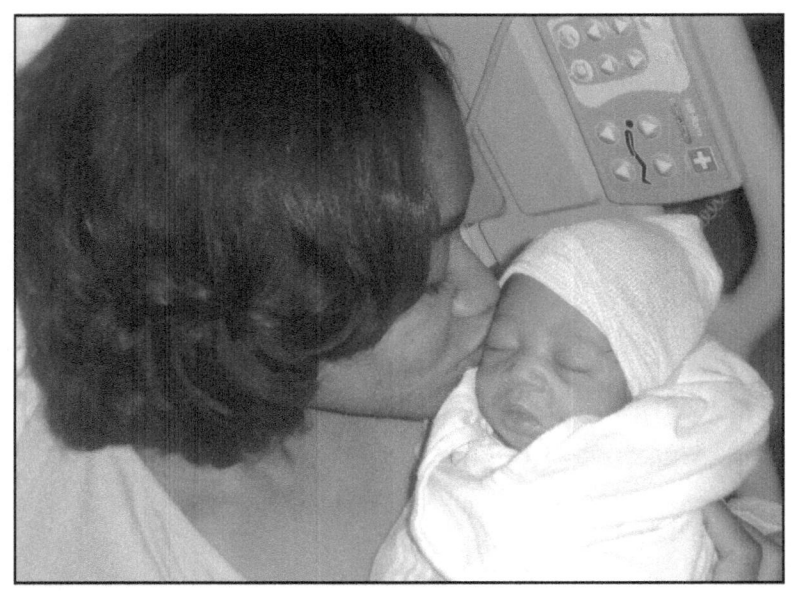

The Antidote

I hated women, so I wanted a little boy.

"Girls are too catty," I used to say.

They hurt me in the past, so I wanted male offspring.

God heard the ache behind the request and found the solution.

The sonogram showed clear as day her female parts.

The doctor confirmed it as she passed through my female parts.

I kissed her and forgave all women.

She was the remedy for my pain.

My little girl.

Her Kiss

For days, I lay exhausted after restless nights of worry.
I ran at your commands and tried to satisfy you.
I sought your comfort and tried to please you,
But your smiles were not for me.

"It was just gas or some seraphim whispering," some said.
But, I waited for my smiles.
In turn, you cried with no requests.
I searched for the answer and came back perplexed.
Your cries left me in a whirlwind of frustration.

One day, after an hour of your tears, I fell apart with you in my
arms.
I prayed for your comfort until I realized my tears were alone.
I looked down, and your lips were turned up at the ends.
Your eyes were almond-shaped, and I saw you grin.

In response, I laughed hysterically,
And a gurgle in your belly told me that you joined me.
I brought your lips to mine, and you opened your mouth,
And a little of your breast-milk–filled saliva crept out.
My first kiss from a girl, and I was in heaven.
Now, I hum to you during the tear-filled hours, waiting for the
next moment of your smile.

Picture Perfect

Your father's eyes and your mother's smile,
Your grandfather's nose and your grandmother's laugh,
You are a mixture of all the good in those around you,
And that makes you great.

Your mother's chin and your daddy's hair,
Your mommy's lips and your father's hands;
Your face is exactly the way I pictured it,
And that makes you picture perfect.

You are my little girl and your daddy's baby.
You are you granddaddy's "boobie" and your grandmother's
pudding.
You are my little pumpkin and everyone's sweetheart,
And that makes you loved more than you can imagine.

Compliments

"She's adorable," they all say in unison.
I try to act humble and thank them for the compliment,
But I know that it's true.

"She should be on a magazine cover," they shout across the store.
I try to act surprised, and I smile as if it's the first time I've heard that,
But I hear it every day.

"She's such a good baby," they say in a whisper in the church pew.
I smile and nod my head to tacitly reply in gratitude.
I try to act coy and hold you nonchalantly,
But I know how wonderful you are.

The truth is that I tell you every day.
I wake up and kiss your pretty face.
You are beautiful, little girl, and a good baby too.
Those are just two small reasons that I love you.

Desires of a Working Mother

I never wanted to be a housewife.
That life seemed boring to me.
Folding laundry and watching soap operas—
That's not where I wanted to be.

I never wanted to stay at home.
Life should be full.
Palmolive-stained hands can make that difficult.

Then, I saw your face.
Your warm smile engulfed my soul.
My ambition was to love you.
Your happiness became my goal.

Now, I'll dream of your eyes.
At work, I'll strain to remember your scent.
Tears fall as I walk out of the door,
Dreading the time away from you.

My thoughts linger on your face,
And tears fall to the floor.
I kiss your lips and hold your sweet breath,
So that I can make it through the day.

My job will require my thoughts,
But my little girl has my heart.

Will you know how much I want to be with you?
Please don't cry for long.
Before you know it, I'll be home.

Colors of a Woman

As a child, I was sky blue
Like a clear summer sky,
Pregnant with chances and
Laughing because there was nothing to cry about.

In puberty, my soft blue skies met rain clouds
As I became conscious of all my flaws.
I hid from myself and I listened to a voice—
The voice within me that tore me to pieces.

By adolescence, I was a mixture of bipolar patterns.
I was hot pink with passion and red with ideas.
Then, I was black midnight when depression came.
It came to suffocate my dreams.

Finally, adulthood came to clean up my tie-dyed world.
It brought bright hues of yellow to propose a new life.
Motherhood brought sights and sounds of a fresh, green spring.
A spring of life brought a reason to beam with happiness.

Now, I worry about her hues.
So, I will offer a plethora of colors—
All with love as a base.
She will not wallow in blacks and grays
The whole rainbow will be her domain.

About the Author

Shannon Johnson is an educator in the Baltimore County Public School system where she has taught for five years. She graduated Magna Cum Laude with a B.A. in English from the University of Maryland Baltimore County and with a Masters of Education from Goucher College in Maryland. Of all of her accomplishments, she is the most proud of her success as a wife and mother, which sparked her desire to publish a book of poetry about womanhood.

She has been writing poetry for 15 years and is passionate about the art form. As an English teacher, Ms. Johnson's goal is to help her students become wordsmiths who use language to change the world. As a woman, she is taking her own advice and has spent several years crafting a book of poetry about the lives of women.

About the book

The Colors of a Woman is a book of poetry that spans the course of a woman's lifetime. The book starts in middle childhood and ends at motherhood. The goal of the book is to uncover the emotions of a girl's transition into adulthood and to showcase the plethora of moods and feelings that women encounter in their relationships with their friends, family members, lovers, God, and themselves. The Colors of a Woman represents the array of hues that are reflected in a woman's emotional rollercoaster known as life.

www.ingramcontent.com/pod-product-compliance
Lightning Source LLC
Chambersburg PA
CBHW021230280526
45784CB00005B/2041